WIF

A Guide to the Top WiFi Auditing Toolkit

Darren Kitchen

Hak5 Founder

WiFi Pineapple Creator

Hak5 LLC, 548 Market Street #39371, San Francisco, CA 94104

WIFI PINEAPPLE
A GUIDE TO THE TOP
WIFI AUDITING TOOLKIT

Copyright © 2017 Hak5 LLC

All rights reserved. This book or any portion thereof may not be reproduced or used in any manner whatsoever without the express written permission of the publisher except for the use of brief quotations in a book review.

Information contained in this book is sold without warranty, either express or implied. Neither the author, nor Hak5 LLC, and its dealers and distributors will be held liable for any damages caused or alleged to be caused directly or indirectly by this book.

International Standard Book Number:
ISBN-13: 978-0-9983732-6-3
Printed in the United States of America
First Printing: November, 2017

Hak5 LLC
548 Market Street #39371
San Francisco, CA 94104

www.Hak5.org
eef5204d6a

CONTENTS

1. PINEAPPLE WHAT?   07

2. WIFI AUDIT WORKFLOW   11

3. BASICS OF WIFI OPERATION   17

4. THE PINEAP SUITE   31

5. HARDWARE OVERVIEW   35

6. WIFI PINEAPPLE SETUP   39

7. SETUP FROM ANDROID   47

8. CONNECTING TO THE INTERNET   51

9. THE WEB INTERFACE   59

10. WIFI PINEAPPLE MODULES   65

11. SHELL ACCESS AND UPGRADES   73

About the Author

Darren Kitchen is the founder of Hak5, the award winning Internet television show inspiring hackers and enthusiasts since 2005. Breaking out of the '90s phone phreak scene, he has continued contributing to the hacker community as a speaker, instructor, author and developer of leading pentesting tools.
darren.kitchen

About the Developer

Sebastian Kinne has led software development at Hak5 since 2011. His background in embedded systems and reverse engineering has been instrumental in the success of the WiFi Pineapple, the popular WiFi auditing tool. As an instructor and speaker on WiFi security, chances are he's sniffed your packets in a demo or two.
sebkinne.com

About the Editor

Shannon Morse is Hak5's host, producer, and editor. Her focus is on security, technology, and DIY for hackers and consumers alike. Shannon is an advocate for women in tech and she welcomes beginners with her easy to understand tutorials.
snubsie.com

About the Artist

Taz Bedevilled is a South African Illustrator/Graphic Artist. She has a degree in Fine Arts and has worked in the industry since 2012. Aside from freelancing, when she gets a quiet moment she enjoys working on her personal projects, such as the web comic: Avocat & His Guac-Rocket.
tazbedevilled.com

Introduction

Since 2008 the WiFi Pineapple has made a name for itself as the go-to tool for WiFi auditing, partly due to its ease of use and partly due to its immense versatility as a hack-anything, hack-anywhere platform. Over the past several years the tool has matured considerably, both in features, usability and purpose-built hardware design. While the intuitive web-based user interface simplifies even the most advanced attacks, there are a number of nuances which may be ambiguous to newcomers. This book aims to provide operational clarity while highlighting wireless auditing best practices with the WiFi Pineapple.

What this book covers

This book takes a practical approach to wireless auditing with the WiFi Pineapple. Sections build on one another beginning with some of the fundamentals of WiFi operation and the theory behind WiFi Pineapple based attacks. The various features and operation are outlined from setting up a fresh out of the box WiFi Pineapple on through gathering intelligence, performing your first audit, setting up a remote deployment, installing modules and keeping up to date with the latest firmware releases. Responsible operation and wifi auditing workflows are emphasized throughout.

Who should read this book

You should read this book if you are a penetration tester, systems administrator, software engineer or other IT professional looking to gain knowledge about the WiFi Pineapple and how to use it to audit WiFi infrastructure and the applications that transit these networks. A moderate technical expertise is appreciated, such as general familiarity with the Linux terminal.

What you need for this

This book covers the 6th generation WiFi Pineapple series - the WiFi Pineapple NANO and its dual-band counterpart the WiFi Pineapple TETRA. The sections of this book are intended to be instructional - so follow along at your own pace.

Disclaimer

The WiFi Pineapple is a wireless penetration testing tool for authorized network auditing and security analysis purposes only where permitted and subject to local and international laws where applicable. Users are solely responsible for compliance with all laws of their locality. Hak5 LLC, WiFi Pineapple developers and affiliates claim no responsibility for unauthorized or unlawful use.

Feedback

WiFi Pineapple development, both software and hardware, are influenced by feedback from the community at large. Our goal is to develop a robust WiFi auditing platform capable of adapting to the ever changing wireless landscape. Similarly this book seeks to grow along with this tool, and as such feedback is immensely important. For general comments and suggestions, please reach out to us at *book@hak5.org*.

1
Pineapple What?

The WiFi Pineapple is a powerful and flexible wireless auditing platform. The project is a combination of continuously evolving hardware, software and modules. It caters to and is supported by a passionate and creative community of penetration testers, systems administrators and wireless enthusiasts.

With each generation, the hardware is designed to take advantage of the best available wireless components of the day. The hardware continues to grow as the user experience is refined and components are updated to respond to the ever changing wireless landscape.

The firmware is engineered alongside the hardware to fully exploit 802.11 protocols. Comprising both the embedded Linux base as well as the web-based user interface, it's in continuous development with free updates delivered over the air.

To further enhance the platform the firmware is designed with an API which enables add-on modules. Modules extend the functionality by providing additional tools and exploits to take advantage of the platform. They can be downloaded and installed over the air from the web interface. In fact, every WiFi Pineapple component is a module which can be updated from the web interface.

What does it do?

Being a versatile Linux-based wireless auditing platform in development since 2008, it does many things. That said, it is best known for it's ability to passively gather intelligence, target and track WiFi enabled devices and effectively deploy a rogue access point for man-in-the-middle attacks.

Rogue Access Point?

The WiFi Pineapple can be deployed as an extremely effective rogue access point. This is done by thoroughly mimicking the preferred wireless networks of client devices such as laptops, phones and tablets.

For convenience, modern WiFi enabled devices automatically connect to networks for which they have previously joined. Over the years the ways in which devices connect to these preferred networks has changed, and throughout the WiFi Pineapple has stayed effective at capturing these clients using its custom PineAP suite.

As an example, this means that a targeted laptop which has previously connected to an airport WiFi network may automatically connect to the penetration testers WiFi Pineapple thinking it is the legitimate network in its preferred network list. Once the targeted device joins the WiFi Pineapple

Pineapple What?

network as a client, it poises the auditor in the position as the man-in-the-middle.

Man-in-the-middle?

Network connections are made up of many nodes. When you browse the web from home, for instance, your traffic goes through many "hops". From your laptop to your wireless access point, your modem and numerous routers between your ISP and the web server of the site you're accessing - your traffic in the form of packets is handed off to a variety of equipment down the chain.

Any node between you and the destination can be considered a man-in-the-middle, in a way, but the term itself generally refers to an attack. This is where an untrusted third party is poised in such a way as to eavesdrop on the connection. An attacker setup as a man-in-the-middle can both monitor and manipulate the traffic down the line.

Original Connection

New Connection

It's a powerful place to be as a penetration tester. The closer you can get in-line to the target, the more successful your attack may become. With the WiFi Pineapple deployed as a rogue access point targeting the individual of interest in an audit, this poises you, the auditor, as the first hop in the chain.

How can the WiFi Pineapple help my pentest?

With an emphasis on responsible auditing within the scope of engagement, the WiFi Pineapple can be used to passively gather intelligence, as well as actively capture clients in order to monitor and manipulate traffic. Modules such as Evil Portal can be deployed to effectively harvest credentials or inject malware onto targeted devices. When used in conjunction with typical tools of the trade, the WiFi Pineapple can easily integrate into your pentest workflow.

As more organizations embrace Bring Your Own Device (BYOD) policies, endless possibilities emerge for the penetration tester. The focus shifts from breaking into the network to *becoming the network*.

2

WiFi Audit Workflow

Any successful engagement requires careful planning and execution. While every scenario differs, this basic workflow outlines the procedures most commonly followed during a WiFi audit. As guidelines they provide insight into responsible best practices.

The goal may be to harvest credentials from the client using a phishing page tailored to the organization, either by DNS poisoning attack or captive portal. It may be to deploy malware such as a reverse shell. Or perhaps it's simply to passively monitor client traffic. Depending on the client device, you may even want it connected to your WiFi Pineapple network in order to attempt a remote exploit. In any case, the typical strategy is to snare a specific target - that is to get the client device of interest to connect to your WiFi Pineapple so that a payload may be delivered.

Pre-Engagement Interactions

A crucial first step is to determine the scope and rules of engagement. This is extremely important since you'll be using a shared spectrum, and ensuring zero collateral damage is key. The more you can obtain up front from the organization about their wireless network and any key targets, the better. Determine how many wireless networks are in operation and whether there is a guest network.

Moreover you'll want to familiarize yourself with any bring your own device (BYOD) policy. For instance, say the organization employs software engineers with high level access to the company infrastructure. Find out if snaring these clients are on the table, and if possible obtain the WNIC MAC addresses of the key individuals.

Intelligence Gathering

The more you can learn about the organization's facilities and its employees, the higher the likelihood of success. Remember, it's not just the company's network infrastructure we're interested in as much as it is the associated staff. What wireless devices do they use? To what other networks do they connect? Do they travel? Do they use guest networks at client sites?

The WiFi Pineapple reconnaissance module facilitates Open Source Intelligence (OSINT) - that is the practice of gathering and analyzing publicly available information sources. It provides the auditor with a big picture of the WiFi landscape, with hooks to the PineAP suite to execute on actionable intelligence.

WiFi Audit Workflow

Vulnerability Analysis

Once initial intelligence has been gathered, one must analyze vulnerabilities. Identify potentially vulnerable targets within the scope of engagement. Are these client devices transmitting probe requests? Are they general or directed at a specific access point? What SSIDs can you determine from their preferred network list? Are they associated to an access point? Are they susceptible to a deauth attack?

Once vulnerabilities have been identified they can be validated. Add the in-scope targets to the allow filter and test them against the available PineAP attacks. Do they connect to your WiFi Pineapple? Do they stay connected?

Exploitation

With in-scope targets identified and validated, the auditor can proceed to exploitation. This will vary greatly depending on the goal of the attack. If it is to capture network traffic for analysis, the tcpdump module may be most appropriate. If it is to harvest credentials from a captive portal using social engineering techniques, the Evil Portal module may be your best bet. In any case, exploitation comes down to setting up the attack, testing the attack, then finally executing it on the given targets.

It is in this phase that careful consideration is put towards tailoring the attack to the targeted individuals and ensuring proper filtering to limit collateral damage.

Post Exploitation

You've successfully obtained associations from your targeted individuals and executed your exploit - be it phishing, sniffing, remote exploit, etc. Now what? Depending on the engagement you may wish to set up persistent remote access in order to maintain a connection with these clients. Or you may have obtained credentials useful in pivoting your attack into the organization's network. By integrating with other popular penetration testing frameworks, the WiFi Pineapple may play the important a role of maintaining your layer 3 network access to these clients throughout the course of the audit.

Reporting

At the conclusion of the WiFi audit the organization will most likely require a report. While the executive level report regarding business impact and bottom line will require a human touch, the technical aspects of this report may be generated by the WiFi Pineapple reporting module. Further the PineAP reports may be analyzed using scripts to determine trends within the organization and its workforce.

In an ongoing WiFi audit, the reporting module may be configured to continuously provide the penetration tester with reports by email at set intervals.

PineAP Workflow

With this basic WiFi auditing guidelines in mind, one may look at the workflow in terms of the PineAP suite and its accompanying modules. The procedures followed with regards to the WiFi Pineapple may look like the following:

Recon - Gather actionable intelligence about the wireless landscape. This module provides a dashboard for quickly identifying potential targets, and interfacing with the filtering and capturing capabilities of the PineAP suite.

Filter - Limiting the scope of engagement is key to a successful audit. Nobody wants collateral damage, so CYA and ensure that only permitted client devices are acquired.

Log - A plethora of actionable intelligence can be passively acquired by logging client device probe requests and associations. Logging is key to successful analysis.

Analyze - What in-scope targets are associated? Which are transmitting probe requests? General or directed? Can you determine the client devices preferred network list?

Capture - A pool of preferred network names are captured, either automatically from nearby probe requests or manually, to the SSID pool. A well curated and targeted SSID pool can be thought of as the sweet, sweet honey of the hot-spot honey-pot.

Prepare - Will you be passively collecting data for analysis? Setup the tcpdump module. Will you be social engineering with a captive portal? Develop the tailored phishing page. Prepare the attack before executing.

Test - Does the attack work as expected? What interaction is required by the client? Test with your own devices before executing.

Broadcast - Advertising the SSID pool to either all nearby devices or specifically targeted devices is an active way of attracting a potential client.

Associate - Finally with filters set for specific targets and a tailored attacked prepared you are ready to allow associations.

Deauthenticate - When permitted, a well placed deauthentication frame may encourage a device to disconnect from their currently associated network and join the WiFi Pineapple. Ensure first that this technique is within the rules of engagement.

Monitor / Manipulate - Capturing traffic for analysis? Set the appropriate modules to log. Manipulating traffic? This is where it pays to get creative with captive portals, DNS spoofing and the like.

Report - What was vulnerable? What wasn't? The PineAP log will show. Further analysis will highlight trends. Compile these for the technical aspects of your report.

Conclusion

A thoughtfully planned and executed WiFi audit is possible by using a number of modules available to the WiFi Pineapple. When used in conjunction with popular penetration testing frameworks the audit will have the largest impact.

Like most productions, the more time spent in the planning stages the higher the likelihood of success. Nobody wants a messy audit. Spend the time to gather intelligence and carefully plan the attack. Going in guns blazing will increase the chances of collateral damage. It cannot be emphasized enough the importance of filtering and tailoring an attack specific to in-scope targets.

While the WiFi Pineapple is capable of executing blanket attacks, be mindful of the wireless landscape. It's ever changing. Just because it's free of civilians now doesn't mean it won't change mid-way through the audit. Target. Filter. Tailor. In short, don't be that guy.

3
Basics of WiFi Operation

In order to get the most out of the WiFi Pineapple, it's best to have a basic understanding of some WiFi principals. This will lay the foundation to mastering the PineAP Suite - the WiFi sniffing and injection engine at the core of the WiFi Pineapple. Armed with this knowledge you'll be equipped to execute a responsible and successful wireless audit by following our recommended wireless auditing workflow.

The purpose of this section is not to be all encompassing on the low level operation of the IEEE 802.11 specification lovingly known as WiFi, but rather a crash course in the absolute basics necessary for understanding the operation of PineAP and other WiFi Pineapple components. If you're already a level 11 kung-fu WiFi guru master, feel free to skip ahead.

Radios and Chipsets

Every WiFi radio is a transceiver, meaning it can transmit (TX) and receive (RX) information. Not every radio is created equal, however, as their capabilities may differ significantly. Software support in particular may inhibit an otherwise fine bit of silicon. In particular, modes of operation may be restricted either by hardware or software.

For the most part chipsets from Atheros have excellent support, with a few RaLink and Realtek chipsets having made a name for themselves in the infosec community as well. Radio chipsets typically interface with a computer over a bus like PCI or USB. A WiFi radio is often called a wireless network interface controller (WNIC or Wireless NIC).

On the other hand a SoC (System on a Chip) is a special WiFi chipset which combines the radio with its own CPU. WiFi SoCs, unlike typical x86-based PCs, traditionally run MIPS based CPUs. While lower in clock speed than their PC counterparts, they're specifically optimized for high performance networking. Both the WiFi Pineapple NANO and TETRA operate on Atheros SoCs.

Logical Configurations

WiFi networks can operate in a number of configurations, from point-to-point, point-to-multipoint, and multipoint-to-multipoint.

Point-to-point is simply a network of two. Multipoint-to-multipoint is where any node of the network can communicate with any other and is often called an ad-hoc, peer-to-peer or mesh network.

The most common configuration is point-to-multipoint, where a central access point is host to numerous client devices. This is also known as Infrastructure mode. An example of which might be a wireless router in your home with several laptops, phones, game consoles and the like connected. For the most part, this is the configuration we will be focusing on with the WiFi Pineapple.

Modes of Operation

Most commonly a WiFi radio will operate in one of three modes: Master, Managed, Monitor. Additional modes include ad-hoc, mesh and repeater and are both less common and outside the scope of this guide.

An Access Point (or simply AP) will operate in Master Mode while client devices operate in Managed Mode. Monitor mode, sometimes called RFMON for Radio Frequency MONitor, is a special mode that allows the radio to passively monitor all traffic in the given area.

Keep in mind that not all radios have each of these capabilities and a radio can only operate in one mode at a time.

Protocols

There are several WiFi protocols known by their letter designated IEEE 802.11 specifications, such as 802.11a, 802.11b, 802.11g and 802.11n. Generally their differences are related to frequency (aka band or spectrum), data rate (aka throughput or transfer speed), bandwidth, modulation and range.

Bandwidth is often confused with data rate. While there is often a correlation between greater bandwidth and greater data rate,

19

in terms of radio the bandwidth refers to the difference between the upper and lower frequencies of a given channel as measured in hertz. For example, with the 802.11g protocol the first channel will have a lower frequency of 2.400 GHz and an upper frequency of 2.422 GHz for a total of 22 MHz bandwidth. An 802.11n based network using 40 MHz bandwidth will occupy nearly twice the spectrum as the 22 MHz wide 802.11g channel and similarly achieve a much faster data rate.

Modulation also affects data rate, with the most common modulation type being OFDM or Orthogonal frequency-division multiplexing. In addition to being a mouthful, it's a digital encoding technique used to cram a lot of data on a small amount of spectrum. It's the same technology used in DSL modems and 4G mobile broadband. The important takeaway is that OFDM supersedes the older DSSS modulation technique used in 802.11b.

802.11a and 802.11b were the first mainstream WiFi protocols, introduced in 1999. 802.11a operates in the 5 GHz band with speeds up to 54 Mbps while 802.11b operates in the 2.4 GHz band with speeds only up to 11 Mbps. These networks are more rare to find, though when they are it's typically indicative of aging infrastructure.

Nowadays 802.11g and 802.11n are more commonly found with data rates up to 54 Mbps and 150 Mbps respectively. Both operate in the 2.4 GHz band with the latter capable of operating in the 5 GHz band as well.

An important thing to consider about protocols is that WiFi radios operating on newer protocols almost always contain backwards compatibility, so an access point using the 802.11g standard may be just as enticing to a client device capable of using the newer 802.11n standard.

Channels and Regions

Radio spectrum is divided up into channels. In the 2.4 GHz spectrum there are 14 channels, with channels 1, 6, 11 and 14 being non-overlapping. As described above in terms of bandwidth, the first channel in the 802.11g protocol begins at 2.400 GHz and ends at 2.422 GHz for a total bandwidth of 22 MHz. The first channel is then described as being centered at 2.412 GHz.

Channel availability is determined by region, with North America only having legal use of channels 1-11 while Europe and most of the world may use channels 1-13. Japan is special and gets access to all of the channels including 14 all to itself.

The 5 GHz spectrum is much more complicated in regards to bandwidth and channel availability by region with further restrictions on indoor/outdoor use. In the United States the FCC designates U-NII (Unlicensed National Information Infrastructure) bands 1-3 available, with 45 channels in total operating in 20, 40, 80 and 160 MHz bandwidth.

The WiFi Pineapple NANO operates in the 2.4 GHz band while the WiFi Pineapple TETRA operates in both the 2.4 and 5 GHz bands.

It's also important to note that similar to modes of operation, a radio can only occupy one channel at a time. For this reason channel hopping is necessary in order to obtain a complete picture of the given spectrum. For example when performing a

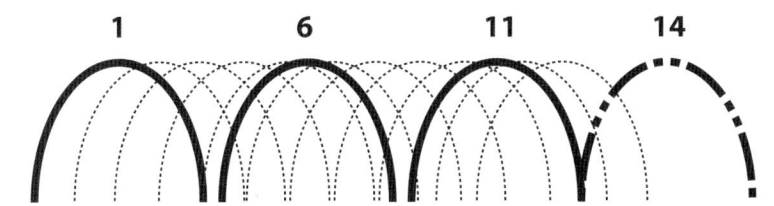

Recon scan, the WiFi Pineapple will switch one of its radios into monitor mode to passively listen on a channel. The radio will take a moment to note any data of interest on each channel before moving on to the next.

Transmit Power

There are four aspects which influence the overall transmission power of a WiFi radio. The first in the chain is what's being transmitted from the chipset or SoC natively. This is typically around 20 dBm or 100 mW and is often expressed in the operating system as txpower.

dBm	Watts
20	100 mW
21	126 mW
22	158 mW
23	200 mW
24	250 mW
25	316 mW
26	398 mW
27	500 mW
28	630 mW
29	800 mW
30	1.0 W
31	1.3 W
32	1.6 W
33	2.0 W
34	2.5 W
35	3.2 W
36	4.0 W

Next is any given amplifier which will boost the source signal before it reaches the antenna. Amplifiers can be onboard, as with the TETRA, or optionally added on as with the NANO. This additional element to the chain is not necessarily integrated with the SoC, and thus may not reflect the actual txpower determined by the operating system.

The final part of the chain is the antenna, which offer the gain as rated in dBi. Antennas coupled with equipment typically have gains in the range of 2 to 5 dBi, as with the NANO and TETRA respectively. Additionally higher gain antennas may be equipped, with 9 dBi being a common size for a standard omnidirectional antenna.

The total output power of this chain is expressed as EIRP, or equivalent isotropically radiated power. The EIRP is calculated by adding the output power of the radio (plus any amplification) in dBm with the gain of the antenna in dBi. For example a 24 dBm (250 mW) radio with a 5 dBi antenna will have a total output power of 29 dBm (800 mW).

Lastly, local regulations will determine the maximum transmission power of any WiFi equipment. For example in the United States the FCC states that a 2.4 GHz point-to-multipoint system may have a maximum of 36 dBm EIRP (4 watts) while point-to-point systems may achieve much higher EIRP.

Stations and Base Stations

Technically speaking in regards to the architecture of any wireless network, each component is referred to as a station (STA). There are two categories of stations in an infrastructure mode WiFi setup – the base station (access point) and station (client). Be aware of this terminology as it may come up in other programs and documentation. Generally the WiFi Pineapple will refer to base stations as their more common name, access point or simply AP, and stations as clients or client devices.

MAC Address

Often called a physical address (PHY addr), the Media Access Control address (MAC address) is a unique identifier assigned to each Network Interface Controller (NIC). Typically this address is "burned" into the ROM of the NIC hardware, though it may be changed via software.

MAC Addresses are formed by six sets of two hexadecimal digits (octets), typically separated by a dash (-) or colon (:) and may be either universally or locally administered. For example, `00:C0:CA:8F:5E:80`.

Universally administered MAC addresses are unique to each NIC manufacturer. The first three octets represent the manufacturer or vendor as its Organizationally Unique Identifier (OUI). In the example above, `00:C0:CA` represents the OUI for ALFA, INC - a popular Taiwanese WiFi equipment maker. OUIs are assigned by the Institute of Electrical and Electronics Engineers, Incorporated (IEEE). The vendor of any particular OUI may be determined by checking the IEEE MAC database, or the Wireshark OUI Lookup Tool.

Locally administered MAC addresses are typically assigned by the network administrator, replacing the universally administered address burned into ROM. For example, one may set their MAC address to `DE:AD:BE:EF:C0:FE`. This is sometimes considered MAC spoofing.

Broadcast address

Often with WiFi networks it is necessary to transmit the same bit of information to all stations. To facilitate this, the WiFi specification includes a special broadcast address. Expressed as the MAC `FF:FF:FF:FF:FF:FF`, transmissions destined to this address are meant for all stations in the vicinity. While normally a WiFi NIC is only concerned with traffic to and from its own MAC address, the default behavior is to also listen for messages bound to the broadcast address. An example of which is a beacon - a frame which advertises the presence of an access point. A beacon sent to broadcast will be "seen" by all stations in the area.

Service Sets and Identifiers

If you've been using WiFi for a while - and if you're reading this book I'll assume you have been - you've undoubtedly run across the term SSID. It's the human readable "network name" associated

Basics of WiFi Operation

with a WiFi Network - like "Joe's Coffee" or "LAX Airport Free WiFi" or depending on your apartment building, perhaps a lewd comment directed toward neighbors. This "network name" is known as the Service Set Identifier. It can be up to 32 characters long and may identify either a Basic or Extended Service Set.

The majority of WiFi networks are Basic Service Sets (BSS). That is to say a single access point with multiple connected clients - be it laptops, tablets, gaming consoles or IoT coffee makers. Every station (both clients and AP) in the BSS are identified by a Basic Service Set Identification (BSSID). The BSSID is derived from the access point's MAC address. Specifically the MAC address of the wireless NIC as the access point may also have an Ethernet Network Interface Controller with its own unique MAC address.

Extended Service Sets are larger WiFi networks whereby multiple access points, each with their own BSSID, all share the same SSID or "network name". For instance a college or corporate campus may require many access points to cover the entire property. In this case the SSID is called an ESSID for Extended Service Set Identification, which facilitates client roaming.

Frames

The meat and potatoes of WiFi. Essentially everything transmitted by a wireless NIC comes in the form of a frame. They are the basic unit of most digital transmissions, and surround or encapsulate packets.

Frame Structure

A typical WiFi frame is broken up into several sections, consisting of a MAC header, payload and frame check sequence.

The **MAC header** contains a Frame Control Field which includes, among other things, the 802.11 protocol version and frame type. Address fields including the BSSID, source and destination are also part of this section.

The **Payload** or frame body contains the actual information (typically a data packet) of either a management or data frame.

The **Frame Check Sequence** (FCS) concludes the frame with a cyclic redundancy check (CRC) sum of the MAC header and payload. This is used to verify the integrity of the frame and is essential to fault tolerance.

802.11 MAC Header

Frame Control	Duration ID	Address 1	Address 2	Address 3	Sequence Control	Address 4	Payload	Frame Check Sequence

30 Bytes   0 - 2312 Bytes   4 Bytes

Frame Types

WiFi frames come in three types, each containing several subtypes; control frames, data frames and management frames,

Control frames simply allow data exchange between stations, with Request to Send (RTS), Clear to Send (CTS) and Acknowledgement (ACK) frames facilitating communication with as little loss as possible. Frame loss is in inherent part of WiFi and control frames are intended to best coordinate shared usage of the available spectrum.

Data frames constitute the majority of WiFi communication, with the payload or frame body containing the actual TCP or UDP packets. Since the data frame has a limit of 2312 bytes, the actual packets may be broken up into many fragments.

Management frames enable WiFi maintenance, such as advertising the presence of an access point as well as connecting to or disconnecting from such access point.

Management Frames

To enable the joining and leaving of a Basic Service Set, management frames contain four basic types; beacon, probe, association, and authentication.

Beacon frames come in only one variety, and advertise the presence of an access point. They contain everything a client needs to know about a network in order to connect, including the SSID, supported data rates, protocol and other parameters pertinent to the APs modulation. Access points regularly transmit beacons, typically several times per second, to the broadcast address.

Beacon frames are essential for network discovery. When a client passively scans for nearby access points, it does so by listening for beacon frames. Typically this is done in conjunction with channel hopping, whereby a client will listen on each channel for a brief period before moving on to the next.

Probe frames further network discovery and come in two variety, probe requests and probe responses. Probe requests are transmitted by clients seeking access points. Probe responses are the access point's replies to these client requests.

When a probe request is transmitted by a client seeking an access point, this is considered active scanning. The client will transmit to the broadcast address either a general probe request or a directed probe request. The former simply asks "what access points are around" while the later specifies the particular SSID for which the client seeks.

The probe response includes all of the basic information about the network also included in the beacon frame.

Association frames come in five forms: the association request, association response, reassociation request, reassociation response, and disassociation. Respectively, these can simply be thought of as "I'd like to be friends", "Ok, we will/won't be friends", "Remember me, I'm your friend", "I do/don't remember you" and "Get lost, friend".

Similar to probe frames, the requests are transmitted by clients while the responses by access points. Disassociation frames in particular are sent by any station wishing to terminate the association. This is the graceful way to ending an association, giving the station a heads up that the conversation is over and allowing it to free up memory in the association table.

Authentication frames are similar to association frames in that they enable the relationship between client and access point to form. Originally only two security states existed for WiFi - Open or Wired Equivalent Privacy (WEP). The later is a broken and deprecated technology which has given way to more secure schemes such as WPA2 and 802.1X. For this reason authentication frames are almost always open, regardless of the security state, with the actual authentication handled by subsequent frames after the station is both authenticated and associated. In this case a client will send an authentication request with the access point sending an authentication response.

Deauthentication frames act similar to disassociation frames and are sent from one station to another as a way to terminate communications. For example, an access point may send a deauthentication frame to a client if it is no longer authorized on its network. When this unencrypted management frame is spoofed by a third party, the technique is often called a deauth attack.

Basics of WiFi Operation

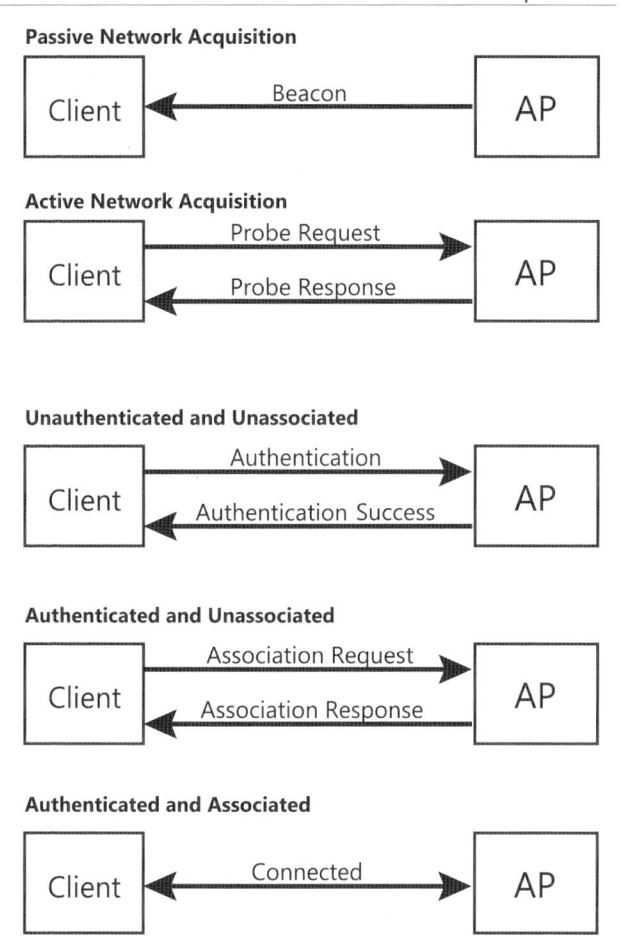

Passive Network Acquisition

Client ← Beacon — AP

Active Network Acquisition

Client → Probe Request → AP
Client ← Probe Response ← AP

Unauthenticated and Unassociated

Client → Authentication → AP
Client ← Authentication Success ← AP

Authenticated and Unassociated

Client → Association Request → AP
Client ← Association Response ← AP

Authenticated and Associated

Client ← Connected → AP

Association and States

With an understanding of management frames, we can explore the states of association. In this example we're looking at the steps necessary for a connection between a client and an open access point.

In the **Unauthenticated and Unassociated** state, the client seeks the access point. This is either done passively by listening to the broadcast address for beacon frames transmitted by the access point, or actively by transmitting a probe request.

29

Once the client has received either a probe response or beacon frame from the access point, it can determine its operating parameters (channel, protocol, data rate, modulation details, etc). The client will then send the access point an authentication frame requesting access. In the case of an open network, the access point will send the client back an authentication frame responding with a success message.

Now the client is **Authenticated and Unassociated**. Next the client will send the access point an association request. The access point will reply with an association response.

If successful, the client will now be **Authenticated and Associated**. At this point any additional security, such as WPA2, may be negotiated. Otherwise in the case of an open network, the usual first network interactions will occur. These are the same as in wired networks, and typically begin with obtaining IP address information from a DHCP server on the host network. In the case of the WiFi Pineapple, the client network is open and the DHCP server will assign new clients with addresses in the 172.16.42.0/24 range.

Frame Injection

By now it should be apparent that much of WiFi operation relies on trust, particularly with regard to the validity of source and destination addresses. Given these values may be spoofed, it's with the technique of frame injection that various attacks may be carried out. Simply put, frame injection is the process of transmitting any WiFi frame desired, regardless of an association with any station. One example may be a beacon frame injected into the air with specific values set to aid the penetration tester. Another may be a deauthentication frame with a spoofed source and destination address. Not all radios and software support this ability. This technique is leveraged by the PineAP suite for a number of attacks using the WiFi Pineapple hardware.

4
The PineAP Suite

At the heart of the WiFi Pineapple is the PineAP suite. It's the intelligent sniffing and injection engine built alongside the custom WiFi Pineapple hardware to fully exploit the 802.11 protocol. PineAP is the software that performs recon, analyzes traffic, captures probes and broadcasts beacons, and enables client device tracking and associations as well as deauthentication - just to name a few. It's built with profiling and filtering capabilities to help identify targets and keep audits limited to the scope of engagement.

While it can operate in both passive and active modes, it's most well known for its ability to snare client devices in its role as a rogue access point. With clients captured, the WiFi Pineapple puts the auditor in the position of the man-in-the-middle. From this vantage point, additional WiFi Pineapple modules and integration with typical pentest tools can be leveraged for a variety of attacks.

Throughout this book we'll dive into each of the major PineAP features and how to make the most of them. Let's first familiarize ourselves with components of the suite in general.

Allow Associations - When enabled, Client devices will be allowed to associate with the WiFi Pineapple through any requested SSID. E.g. If a Client device sends a Probe Request for SSID "example" the WiFi Pineapple will acknowledge the request, respond and allow the Client device to associate and connect to the WiFi Pineapple network. This feature works in conjunction with Client and SSID filtering. When disabled; clients will not be allowed to associate. Before the evolution of the PineAP suite with the 5th generation WiFi Pineapple, this feature was known as Karma.

Log Probes - When enabled, the PineAP suite will continuously sniff for Probe Request frames from nearby client devices. This feature provides information for analysis from the Logging view.

Log Associations - When enabled, Client Associations to the WiFi Pineapple will be logged. This feature provides information for analysis from the Logging view. If disabled, Associations will not be logged and may not appear in the SSID column from the Clients view.

PineAP Daemon - This daemon must be enabled in order to use the Beacon Response, Capture SSIDs to Pool and Broadcast SSID pool features. The PineAP Daemon will coordinate the appropriate actions based on Source and Target MAC settings as well as the Beacon Response and SSID Broadcast intervals.

This feature requires dedicated access to the `wlan1` radio and cannot be used in conjunction with the WiFi Client Mode feature using `wlan1` to provide Internet access to the WiFi Pineapple. However, if using a tertiary USB WiFi adapter configured as `wlan2`, PineAP and WiFi Client Mode work well together.

The PineAP Daemon must be enabled and PineAP Settings must be saved before the associated features will be available.

Beacon Response - When enabled, targeted beacons will be transmitted to Client devices in response to a Probe Request with the appropriate SSID. These beacons will not be transmitted to broadcast, but rather specifically to the device making the probe request. This prevents the beacon from being visible to other devices. If Allow Associations is enabled and the Client device associates with the WiFi Pineapple, then targeted Beacon Responses will continue to transmit to the Client device for a period of time. Beacon Responses will use the Source MAC setting, which is also shared with the Broadcast SSID Pool feature. The Beacon Response Interval will dictate how frequently to transmit.

Capture SSIDs to Pool - When enabled, the sniffer will save the SSID data of captured Probe Requests to the SSID Pool. This passive feature benefits the Broadcast SSID Pool feature. The SSID Pool may also be managed manually.

Broadcast SSID Pool - When enabled, the SSID Pool will be broadcast as beacons using the Source MAC and Target MAC settings at the interval specified. During the evolution of the PineAP suite this feature was known to the WiFi Pineapple Mark V as "Dogma" as a compliment to "Karma".

Source MAC - By default, this is the MAC address of wlan0 on the WiFi Pineapple. This is the interface for which associations may be allowed and also hosts the Management Access Point. The MAC address of wlan0 may be changed from the Networking view. This MAC address may be set to that of a secondary WiFi Pineapple if desired. In this configuration multiple WiFi Pineapples may be deployed concurrently, with one configured to allow associations.

Target MAC - By default, this is the broadcast MAC address FF:FF:FF:FF:FF:FF. Frames transmitted to the broadcast address will be seen by all nearby Client devices. Setting the Client MAC address will target PineAP features at the single device. Similar to Beacon Response, only SSIDs Broadcast from the Pool will be visible to the targeted Client device. When used in conjunction with Filtering, this feature enables precision device targeting.

Broadcast SSID Pool Interval - Specifies the Interval in which to Broadcast SSIDs from the Pool. Aggressive will transmit beacons from the SSID pool more frequently, albeit with a higher CPU utilization.

Beacon Response Interval - Specifies the Interval in which to transmit Beacon Responses. Similar to Broadcast SSID Pool Interval, the aggressive mode will transmit more frequently while requiring a higher CPU utilization.

Save Active Config as Default - From the Configuration menu, Saving the active config as the default on Boot will remember the saved PineAP features and settings for use on the next boot cycle.

SSID Pool - Populated automatically when the Capture SSID Pool feature is enabled. May also be added manually using the text field and Add button. Similarly, clicking a listed SSID will populate the text field allowing for the removal of the entry using the Remove button. From the SSID Pool Menu, Clear SSID Pool will remove all entries.

5
Hardware Overview

The WiFi Pineapple hardware is a purpose built wireless auditing platform, combining versatile and convenient components to address the needs of the penetration tester. With each iteration of the WiFi Pineapple, hardware changes are made to refine the user experience, address the needs of the penetration tester and adapt to the ever changing wireless landscape.

The Mark I through Mark III were very similar, all being based on an Atheros AR2315 SoC. The Mark IV was the last single-radio design, with additional radios being added via USB. This led to development of the first fully custom WiFi Pineapple - the Mark V. This model included both Atheros and onboard Realtek radios and introduced the PineAP suite.

The 6th generation hardware builds on experience gained from the Mark V with a refined user experience that emphasizes power, convenience and workflow. The 6th generation line is split between two models covering various use cases.

Both **WiFi Pineapple NANO** and **WiFi Pineapple TETRA** feature two discrete Atheros radios designed to fully exploit the PineAP suite. They run similar firmware versions, with minor nuances suited to their particular hardware. Their designs are centered around mobile auditing and long term deployments respectively, though they're both fully capable of either scenario.

The NANO emphasizes portability with its dongle-like design. It's capable of being powered from a laptop's USB port or a USB battery pack, such as in its tactical edition configuration. This makes it a convenient solution for auditing on the go. There's also no cable clutter when using the WiFi Pineapple NANO since its USB plug doubles as both power source and USB Ethernet adapter. Storage is expandable via MicroSD card. The female USB port can be host to mass storage, GPS, Ethernet adapters, additional WiFi radios, some USB modems and Android devices.

Specifications
CPU: 400 MHz MIPS Atheros AR9331 SoC. **Memory**: 64 MB DDR2 RAM. **Disk**: 16 MB ROM + MicroSD). **Wireless**: Atheros AR9331 (`wlan0`) + Atheros AR9271 (`wlan1`), both IEEE 802.11 b/g/n. **Ports**: (2) RP-SMA Antenna, Ethernet over USB (ASIX AX88772A) USB 2.0 Host, MicroSD card reader. **Power**: USB 5V 1.5A. Includes USB Y-Cable.

The TETRA addresses the need for a high power dual-band solution. It features two Atheros radios operating in both the 2.4 GHz and 5 GHz bands. The high gain antennas coupled with the four onboard amplifiers deliver immense output power. Like a traditional WiFi Access Point, it features a wired Ethernet port. Similar to the WiFi Pineapple NANO, it hosts an internal USB Ethernet adapter making its connection to a host computer convenient with a single USB cable. The command prompt is conveniently accessed via the onboard UART, which provides a serial connection over USB. Power can be provided by either a traditional 12V wall outlet or by USB. The USB power option is best suited to computers capable of providing adequate amperage, like desktops and workstation laptops. Fast flash storage is onboard, while additional storage as well as other accessories may be connected by USB.

Specifications
CPU: 533 MHz MIPS 74K Atheros AR9344 SoC. **Memory**: 128 MB DDR2 RAM. **Disk**: 2 GB NAND Flash. **Wireless**: Atheros AR9344 + Atheros AR9580, both IEEE 802.11 a/b/g/n with quad integrated skybridge amplifiers and included 5 dBi antenna for a high 29 dBm gain EIRP. **Ports**: (4) SMA Antenna, RJ45 Fast Ethernet, Ethernet over USB, Serial over USB, USB 2.0 Host, 12V/2A DC Power. **Power**: Requires 18W. Accepts power from any combination of sources; DC Barrel Port, USB ETH port, USB UART port. AC wall adapter for stationary deployment and USB Y cable for mobile deployment included.

Power Considerations

Since the beginning of the WiFi Pineapple, careful consideration is put into powering options. The original Mark I for instance included a soldered-on 4xAA battery pack. Versatility in powering the device has led to some creative deployment options and overall usability.

WiFi Pineapple NANO

The WiFi Pineapple NANO requires 9W for stable operation under high load. This figure accounts for a 2.5W USB accessory in addition to maximum utilization of the CPU, SD card and radios. Power is provided from the male USB type A plug. A USB Y cable is provided with the WiFi Pineapple NANO for use with devices incapable of providing sufficient amperage from a single USB port.

WiFi Pineapple TETRA

The WiFi Pineapple TETRA requires 18W for normal stable operation. While the device may function under minimal load with less power, system instability may occur during peak load.

Power may be provided to the device by any combination of USB UART, USB ETH, or 12V DC ports. The 12V DC port accepts a standard IEC 60130-10:1971 type A connector with 5.5 mm OD, 2.1 mm ID (center positive). This is the common barrel plug used in all previous generation WiFi Pineapples.

The UART and ETH ports on the WiFi Pineapple TETRA will accept power from combined USB sources, such as from computers, wall adapters or batteries via USB Y cables. There is no risk of providing too much power from standard 5 volt USB sources as the WiFi Pineapple TETRA will only draw as much amperage as needed.

Most modern computers are capable of providing the necessary amperage from their USB ports to power the WiFi Pineapple TETRA using two USB Y cables. Older computers and many netbooks however may not provide enough continuous current for stable operation.

When calculating total power in wattage, multiply the voltage and amperage. USB sources are always 5V and may vary in amperage depending on configuration. Many older USB 2.0 ports are limited to the 500mA specification while newer USB 3.0 ports can deliver 900mA and above. Typically notebook computers with USB charge ports (indicated in yellow, red or by a lightning icon) will provide even higher amperage.

6
WiFi Pineapple Setup

Once you've unboxed your new WiFi Pineapple, be it a TETRA or NANO, you'll want to load it up with the latest firmware. Out of the box neither edition of the WiFi Pineapple run any version of the penetration testing software, but rather a locked down stager will boot. The stager enables a secure update, ensuring that you're always running the latest firmware version.

The basic setup process is to download the latest firmware, connect the WiFi Pineapple to the host device, browse to the WiFi Pineapple web interface from the host device and follow the on-screen instructions to complete the firmware flashing process.

Setup can be completed from any modern device, as long as it has a web browser and a connection to both the Internet and the WiFi Pineapple. An Ethernet connection to the WiFi Pineapple is preferred as it is the most secure way to complete the setup process.

TL;DR

1. Download the latest firmware from *https://www.wifipineapple.com/downloads*.
2. Power on the device and connect it to your Windows or Linux computer via USB.

   TETRA: Use the AC adapter and connect a USB cable between the PC to the ETH port.
   NANO: Use both leads of the USB-Y adapter to power and connect to the PC.

3. Browse to *http://172.16.42.1:1471* (Only Chrome and Firefox are officially supported)
4. Follow the onscreen instructions to complete setup.

Setup Security

For security reasons, you'll be prompted to press the reset button on your WiFi Pineapple during setup. This authenticates you as having physical access to the device, and thus the most likely owner.

Pressing the reset button when prompted will disable the device's WiFi network, which will have the SSID as "`pineapple_xxxx`" (where xxxx is the last 2 octets of your WiFi Pineapples `wlan0` MAC address). If for whatever reason you cannot complete setup with an Ethernet connection to the WiFi Pineapple, you'll have the option to override this security feature by holding the reset button for 3 or more seconds.

This security feature is intended to authenticate the owner of the device as well as limit any potential attack surface by disabling

WiFi so that only the legitimate owner may connect. There are inherent risks in WiFi after all, and this irony is not lost on the author.

The Reset button is located on the underside of the WiFi Pineapple NANO and on the back of the WiFi Pineapple TETRA.

Setting up the WiFi Pineapple NANO or TETRA in Linux or Windows

Download and verify the latest firmware

Begin by downloading the latest version of the WiFi Pineapple firmware for your device (NANO or TETRA) to your computer from the Downloads page at *https://www.wifipineapple.com/downloads*.

The latest version of the firmware will be listed at the top of the page, along with a download link and SHA256 hash. The filename will be `upgrade-x.x.x.bin` where x.x.x is the version number.

It's always a good idea to check the integrity of the downloaded file, especially with firmware binaries. Check the SHA256 sum of the file and verify that it's identical to the sum listed on the downloads page. If the sums differ, delete the file and try the download again.

Linux: From the terminal, use the sha256sum command. For example, if the `upgrade-x.x.x.bin` file is located in the Downloads folder of your home directory, the command may be `sha256sum ~/Downloads/upgrade-x.x.x.bin`.

Windows: sha256sum isn't native to Windows, though two free open source options are recommended. Either Quick Hash GUI from *https://sourceforge.net/projects/quickhash/* or for the PowerShell savvy, the Get Hashes of Files PS1 script from *https://gallery.technet.microsoft.com/scriptcenter/Get-Hashes-of-Files-1d85de46.*

Power on and connect the WiFi Pineapple
Once the firmware has been downloaded and verified, the next step is to power on and get connected to the WiFi Pineapple.

NANO: Plug the USB Y cable into two USB female host ports on the PC side, and the male USB plug on the WiFi Pineapple NANO side. If only one USB port is available on the PC side, first ensure that it is capable of providing the necessary 9W. Also be sure to use the thicker data end of the USB plug as the thinner pigtail only supplies power from an additional port. See the section on power considerations for details.

TETRA: Plug the wall power adapter into an available AC outlet and the DC barrel port of the WiFi Pineapple TETRA. The wall power adapter supports 50/60 Hz and is adaptable from its standard US plugs for international users. This configuration will provide ideal power for the setup process. Next connect a Micro USB cable between the TETRA port labeled ETH and the computer. If using the USB Y cable provided with the TETRA, note that the thin pigtail on the USB A end is only for providing additional power. See the section on power consideration.

Bootup of the WiFi Pineapple NANO or TETRA will begin as soon as power is applied to the device and will be indicated as complete when the blue LED goes solid. There may be subtle flickering to indicate network activity at this time.

Both the WiFi Pineapple NANO and TETRA include onboard USB Ethernet adapters, which will enumerate as such on the host PC. Driver installation should be automatic on modern Windows and Linux operating systems - otherwise check the Troubleshooting section.

On Linux computers the interface will have either a classic `ethX` name, such as `eth1`, or the newer `enxXXXXXXXXXXXX` style naming convention (where the Xs represent the WiFi Pineapple's Ethernet MAC address).

On Windows computers the interface may simply be named "Ethernet 2" and can be identified by the Device Name. The NANO will enumerate as an "ASIX AX88772A USB2.0 to Fast Ethernet Adapter" while the TETRA will show as a "Realtek USB FE Family Controller".

By default the WiFi Pineapple is setup to offer the PC connected via USB Ethernet an IP address in the `172.16.42.x` range from its DHCP server.

Linux users can verify this by running the ifconfig command from the terminal and checking for an IP address in the `172.16.42.x` range from the Ethernet device associated with the WiFi Pineapple.

Windows users can verify this by running ncpa.cpl from the run line (**Windows Key + R**) and double-clicking the Ethernet adapter associated with the WiFi Pineapple. From the Status window, click Details and check for an IP address in the `172.16.42.x` range.

Browse to the Setup page

With the WiFi Pineapple powered on and connected via USB Ethernet to the host computer, we're ready to browse over to the web interface. While under the hood the WiFi Pineapple is running an embedded Linux operating system, much of the functionality is exposed simply through a web interface. This makes not only management easy, but setup as well.

When managing the WiFi Pineapple from the web interface, it's important to use a well supported browser. Google Chrome and Mozilla Firefox are the only officially supported browsers, though we've seen good results with variants like Chromium and

Iceweasel (the Kali Linux default). Microsoft Internet Explorer is not supported.

From a compatible browser, navigate to *http://172.16.42.1:1471*

Complete the Setup wizard

From the web interface you will be greeted with a WiFi Pineapple logo. When prompted click Continue to begin the setup process. You will be instructed to press the reset button to confirm physical presence, authenticate and disable the WiFi radios. When prompted for the latest software, click "Choose File" and browse to select the `upgrade-x.x.x.bin` file saved from the first step. Finally, click Upgrade to start the firmware flashing process.

At this time the `upgrade-x.x.x.bin` file will be uploaded to the WiFi Pineapple and the firmware will begin to upgrade. This process typically takes 5-10 minutes.

It is important to leave the WiFi Pineapple uninterrupted during the firmware flashing process. If power is interrupted, the device will most certainly become "bricked". This term simply means that it will reside in a non-functioning state. Since the operating system is being written from the `upgrade-x.x.x.bin` file bit by bit, any interruption in power will leave you with a corrupted system.

While certain precautions have been made to ensure that the device is "unbrickable", such as the firmware recovery bootloader discussed in the troubleshooting section of this book, it's always advised to leave a flashing device undisturbed.

WiFi Pineapple Setup

When firmware flashing completes the WiFi Pineapple will reboot, as indicated by a blinking blue LED followed by a solid blue LED. At this point the web browser should automatically redirect to continue with the setup wizard. If this does not occur, you may need to manually refresh the page. The CTRL+SHIFT+R keyboard shortcut of Chrome and Firefox will reload the page while overriding the cache.

When greeted by the web interface, click Get Started. You will be prompted to press the reset button once more in order to authenticate and disable the WiFi radios. Once pressed the setup wizard will automatically continue to prompt for new default settings.

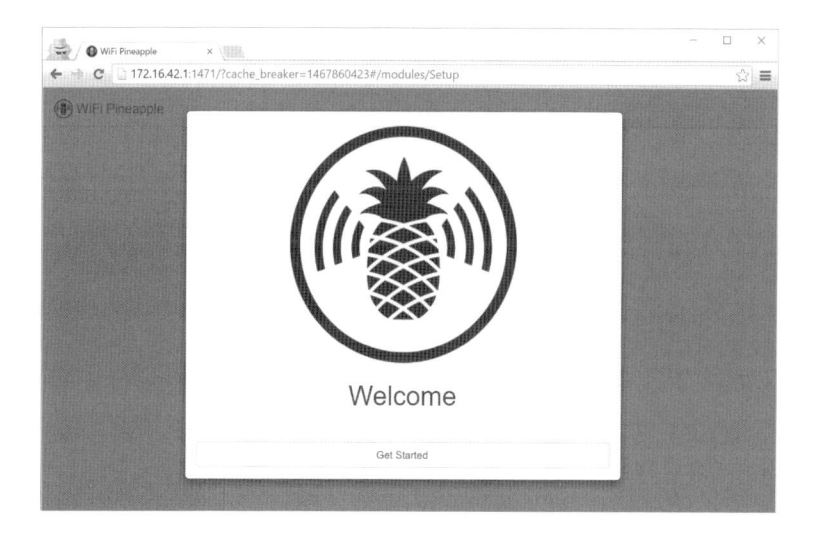

Set a good root password. This will be used to login to the web interface as well as interact with the shell over SSH.

You will also be required to set a Management access point SSID (network name) and WPA2 passphrase. The Management AP is a special access point hosted on the device for the purpose of secure management over WiFi.

After clicking Complete Setup you will be prompted to login for the first time using the root password set previously in this step. Once authenticated you will be greeted with the dashboard.

Congratulations, your WiFi Pineapple is now up and running with the latest version of the firmware!

7
Setup from Android

Setting up a new WiFi Pineapple with an Android device like a smartphone or tablet is very simple. It is best to familiarize yourself with the previous section on setup from Windows and Linux as the process has many similarities.

Download the Latest Firmware

Begin by downloading the latest version of the WiFi Pineapple firmware onto the Android device. From Google Chrome or your browser of choice on the Android device, browse to *https://www.wifipineapple.com/downloads* and be sure to select the appropriate device, either the NANO or TETRA, from the download tab. The latest version will be listed first, so go ahead and tap Download Now, linked just below the change log. A version numbered upgrade.bin file will be saved to the devices Downloads directory.

Install the WiFi Pineapple Connector app
Next install the WiFi Pineapple Connector app onto the Android device from the Google Play Store. This app will simplify the setup process, as well as enable Internet connection sharing and management of your WiFi Pineapple from the Android device in the future. Search "WiFi Pineapple Connector" in the Play Store, or browse to *https://play.google.com/store/apps/details?id=org.hak5.pineappleconnector* from the device's web browser.

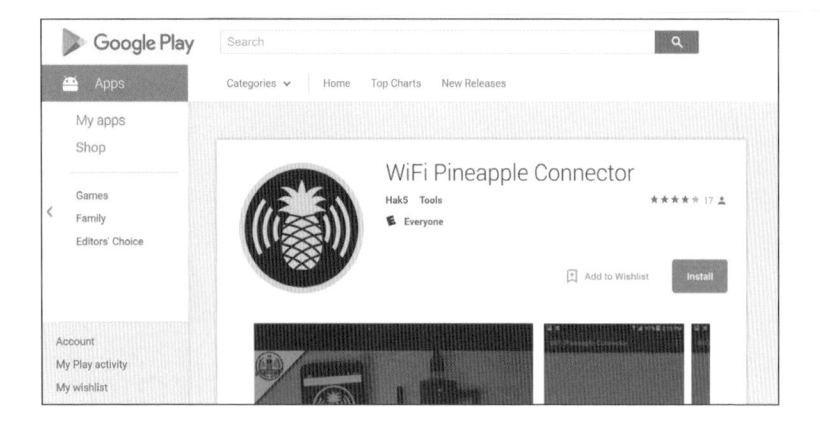

Power on the WiFi Pineapple
Powered on the WiFi Pineapple. TETRA operators use the AC adapter while NANO operators should use a USB power source capable of supplying 9W. See the previous section on power considerations if necessary.

Once fully booted, the blue LED indicator will appear solid. Connect the WiFi Pineapple to the Android device using a data capable USB cable. This is typically a standard Micro USB or USB-C cable on newer devices. Plug the Male A end into the USB host port on the WiFi Pineapple, and the Micro or USB-C end into the Android device.

The female USB host port on the NANO is located opposite the male USB A plug. On the TETRA, the USB host port is located on the back of the device next to the Ethernet jack.

Be sure to use a data capable USB cable, such as the one typically included with the Android device. Note that some USB cables are for charging only, such as the one included with the Pineapple Juice 4000 battery pack.

Enable USB Tethering

From the Android device, open the WiFi Pineapple Connector app. You'll be prompted to enable USB tethering. When asked "Have you enabled USB tethering" tap NO to be taken to the Mobile HotSpot and Tethering settings screen. Tap to enable USB tethering, then tap back to return to the WiFi Pineapple Connector app. This time when asked "Have you enabled USB tethering?" tap YES to continue. The app will then wait for the WiFi Pineapple to make a connection.

At this point you may be prompted to download the latest firmware. Since we've already completed this in the first step, tap to begin setup.

Complete the Setup Wizard

This step is identical to step 4 of the setup process in Windows or Linux as described in the previous chapter. The important differences with Android to note are:

When tapping "Choose File" select the downloaded `upgrade-x.x.x.bin` file by selecting "Documents" then Open From "Recent".

Once you tap Upgrade to start the firmware flashing process you will be notified that USB Tethering will need to be re-enabled after the WiFi Pineapple reboots. This may require the USB cable to be physically disconnected and reconnected. USB Tethering can then be achieved by re-launching the WiFi Pineapple Connector app and once again following the prompts.

8
Connecting to the Internet

The WiFi Pineapple may be used to provide WiFi clients with Internet access. While this may not be necessary for all deployment scenarios, it is commonly configured. There are four basic methods for setting up an Internet connection on the WiFi Pineapple.

1. Wired Internet Connection
2. Internet Connection Sharing
3. USB Tethering from Android
4. WiFi Client Mode

These sections serve as guides to setting up a WiFi Pineapple Internet connection. However, please be advised that this guide cannot cover the infinite possible network configurations.

Wired Internet Connection

The WiFi Pineapple TETRA provides two Ethernet ports. A WAN port via a traditional RJ45 port, as well as a LAN port accessible by its USB ETH port. The USB ETH port connects the host device to the LAN via an onboard Realtek USB Ethernet controller.

The WAN port is connected to `eth0` on the WiFi Pineapple TETRA and by default will attempt to obtain an IP address from DHCP.

The LAN port is connected to `eth1` on the WiFi Pineapple TETRA and hosts the internal DHCP server which will offer an IP address in the `172.16.42.x` range by default.

Note: If Windows does not automatically install the Microsoft WHQL USB Ethernet driver from Windows Update, you may download it from Realtek at *http://goo.gl/rCBXks*

The WiFi Pineapple NANO may be enhanced with wired Ethernet functionality by using a supported USB Ethernet adapter. This accessory, when plugged into the USB Host port on the WiFi Pineapple NANO, will enumerate as `eth1`. Standard network and firewall configuration may apply. See the appropriate `/etc/config` files for details.

Internet Connection Sharing

One of the most popular deployment scenarios is to configure the WiFi Pineapple to share an Internet connection from a personal computer, such as a notebook running Windows or Linux. With the WiFi Pineapple providing its WiFi clients Internet access from the host PC, the penetration tester may then extend MITM functions through desktop applications such as packet analyzers and auditing frameworks.

Ethernet with Windows

By default the WiFi Pineapple is expecting an Internet connection from 172.16.42.42 on its LAN. Connect the WiFi Pineapple LAN port to the Windows PC host. On the NANO this is the male USB A plug. On the TETRA this is the USB ETH port.

- From the Windows Run prompt (keyboard shortcut Windows Key + R) execute `ncpa.cpl`
- Locate the WiFi Pineapple network interface
- For convenience the network interface may be renamed by highlighting it and using the keyboard shortcut F2
- From the Internet connection source (typically a WiFi or Ethernet), right-click the interface and select Properties.
- From the Sharing tab check the box labeled "Allow other network users to connect through this computer's Internet connection" and select the WiFi Pineapple network interface from the drop down menu.
- Click OK
- Right-click the WiFi Pineapple network interface and select Properties
- Select Internet Protocol Version 4 (TCP/IPv4) and click Properties
- Replace the default IP address with `172.16.42.42`
- Click OK
- Click Close

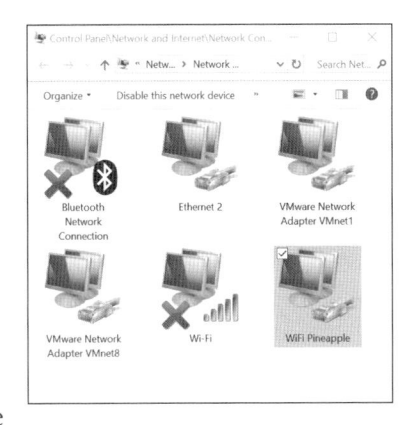

Ethernet with Linux

By default the WiFi Pineapple is expecting an Internet connection from `172.16.42.42` on its LAN. Connect the WiFi Pineapple LAN port to the Linux PC host. On the NANO this is the male USB A plug. On the TETRA this is the USB ETH port.

Once connected, the network connection of the host Linux PC may be forwarded to the WiFi Pineapple using iptables. A free script is available to aid in iptables configuration for most Linux hosts.

To download the script from the terminal, run `wget www.wifipineapple.com/wp6.sh`. Next the script must be made executable, typically by running `chmod +x wp6.sh`. Finally execute the script by running `./wp6.sh`.

The WiFi Pineapple Connector script for Linux offers either guided or manual setup modes. For most the guided setup is advised. Press `G` then follow the onscreen prompts to save the connection settings. Once saved, press `C` to connect.

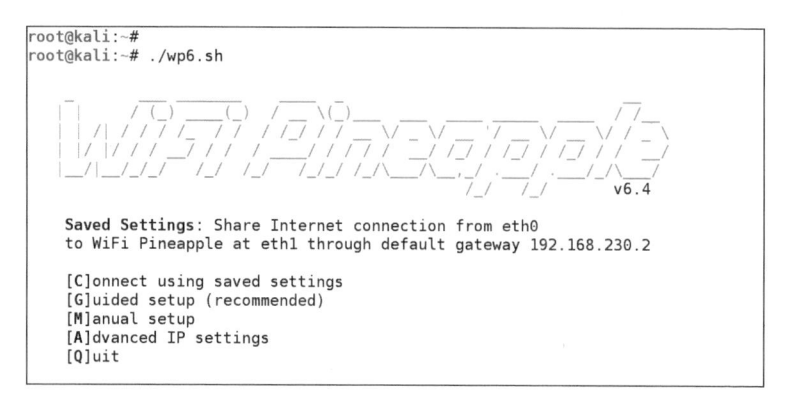

```
root@kali:~#
root@kali:~# ./wp6.sh

 _       ___  _____   _  _____                              _       
| |     / (_)/ ____(_)/ ___ \____  ___  ____ _____  ____  / /__    
| | /| / / // /_  / // /_/ / __ \/ _ \/ __ `/ __ \/ __ \/ / _ \   
| |/ |/ / // __/ / // ____/ / / /  __/ /_/ / /_/ / /_/ / /  __/   
|__/|__/_//_/   /_//_/   /_/ /_/\___/\__,_/ .___/ .___/_/\___/    
                                         /_/   /_/        v6.4     

Saved Settings: Share Internet connection from eth0
to WiFi Pineapple at eth1 through default gateway 192.168.230.2

[C]onnect using saved settings
[G]uided setup (recommended)
[M]anual setup
[A]dvanced IP settings
[Q]uit
```

The WiFi Pineapple Connector script for Linux is provided free of charge for convenience, without warranty, and is not necessary for successful operation of the WiFi Pineapple.

USB Tethering (Android)

The WiFi Pineapple can be provided an Internet connection from many means, including USB Ethernet adapters. Many Android devices have the capability to emulate USB Ethernet adapters, sharing their Internet connections with other devices like notebook computers.

Check to see if your Android device supports this Internet Connection Sharing method by selecting Tethering and Portable Hotspot from the Network section of the Settings application. If the option for USB Tethering exists, your Android device may be capable of sharing its Internet connection with the WiFI Pineapple.

Depending on Android ROM and Carrier restrictions, this feature may be unavailable or require a subscription. To test, plug a data-capable USB cable between the host port on the WiFI Pineapple and the Android device. The USB Tethering option should become available.

Note: The USB cable provided with the Pineapple Juice battery is for charging only and does not support data transfer.

If USB Tethering is supported by the Android device, when enabled it will enumerate on the WiFi Pineapple as a new network interface, usb0, and the WiFi Pineapple will automatically adjust its kernel routing table to use this interface for its Internet access, as well as Internet access for any clients connected to the WiFi Pineapple. Via DHCP, the WiFi Pineapple will receive an IP address on the Android devices internal network (typically 192.168.x.x).

Since the WiFi Pineapple will become a client on the Android devices internal network, it is possible to access the WiFi Pineapple web interface from the Android device if the WiFi Pineapple's IP address is known.

For convenience in accessing the USB Tethering setting, as well as discovering the IP address of the WiFi Pineapple on the Android device's network and browsing to the web interface, a WiFi Pineapple Connector app for Android is provided free of charge from Google Play.

When launching the WiFi Pineapple Connector Android app, you will be prompted to configure tethering. Tapping no will jump to the systems Tethering and Portable Hotspot settings menu, if available. Tap to enable USB Tethering, then tap back. Once enabled, the WiFi Pineapple Connector app will wait for a network connection from the WiFi Pineapple indicating its IP address on the Android devices internal network. Once discovered, the browser will automatically load the web interface.

It's important to better understand what's happening on the WiFi Pineapple end. When USB Tethering is enabled, the Android device will enumerate on the WiFi Pineapple as a new USB Ethernet device. This is similar to how any supported USB Ethernet adapter may be plugged into the WiFi Pineapple. This new USB Ethernet device will be assigned the interface name usb0, similar to how Ethernet devices are named eth0. When the WiFi Pineapple detects the usb0 interface, it will attempt to retrieve an IP address via DHCP. By default Android's USB Tethering functionality will host a DHCP server, offering the connected device an IP address in the 192.168.x.x range. Once the WiFi Pineapple receives an address, it will attempt to establish a connection with the host Android device, periodically sending its IP address as well as status information.

Not all Android devices use the standard USB Tethering API or may block the data transfer from the WiFi Pineapple to the Android device. In this case USB Tethering may be enabled, but the WiFi Pineapple Connector app will be unable to determine the IP address of the WiFi Pineapple and launch the browser automatically. In this case determining the IP address of usb0 on the WiFi Pineapple may be initiated by another means, such as from a serial connection or from another device connected to the WiFi Pineapple over WiFi.

The Android API restricts systematically enabling the USB Tethering function, which is why the WiFi Pineapple Connector app can only jump to the systems Tethering and Portable Hotspot settings menu. This functionality may be achieved on rooted devices by other means.

The WiFi Pineapple Connector app for Android is provided free of charge for convenience, without warranty, and is not necessary for successful operation of the WiFi Pineapple. We strive to make it as convenient as possible, but unfortunately due to differences in ways manufacturers implement the tethering spec, or how carriers lock down certain features, we cannot guarantee all devices will be compatible.

WiFi Client Mode

The WiFi Pineapple may obtain an Internet connection from a nearby access point, such as a traditional wireless router as well as personal hotspots and WiFi tethering from smartphones. While achievable throughput may not be as high as with traditional wired, shared or tethered configurations - WiFi Client Mode provides significant convenience for many deployments.

To begin, first note that while the WiFi Pineapple includes two radios (wlan0 and wlan1), they are both required for PineAP operation. If the second radio (wlan1) is used for Client Mode, PineAP functions may not be used. For this reason the auditor is advised to use an external USB WiFi adapter with a compatible chipset.

Compatible chipsets include RaLink RT2800 devices, as well as some Atheros and RealTek devices. Wireless adapters from *HakShop.com* are certified to work with the WiFi Pineapple.

To enable WiFi Client Mode, navigate to the Networking section of the web interface. From the WiFi Client Mode heading, select the desired interface. When using external USB WiFi adapters, these will be listed as `wlan2` and greater.

With the preferred adapter selected, click Scan to perform a site survey of nearby access points. When the scan completes, a list of Access Points will be available from a drop-down menu.

Selecting an Access Point will display additional information about the base station, such as BSSID, SSID, channel, signal strength, quality and security.

WPA protected Access Points will require a password. With the Access Point selected, and a WPA key entered if required, click Connect. This will instruct the WiFi Pineapple to attempt to associate with the selected network and obtain an IP address from DHCP. Clicking Refresh will identify the WiFi Pineapple IP address on the target network.

Once configured for WiFi Client Mode, the WiFi Pineapple will attempt to connect to the desired Access Point after each boot.

To disconnect and prevent subsequent connections at boot, click the Disconnect button from the WiFi Client Mode section of the Networking page in the web interface.

WiFi Client Mode connection information is stored in the `/etc/config/wireless` configuration file.

The Web Interface

The WiFi Pineapple Web Interface provides convenient access to most WiFi Pineapple functions. It may be accessed by most modern devices (PC, Tablet, Smartphone). Officially supported web browsers include Google Chrome and Mozilla Firefox.

This chapter will explore accessing the web interface, its various elements and navigation as well as some of the sections not specifically addressed by subsequent chapters.

Accessing the Web Interface

To access the Web Interface, first connect to the WiFi Pineapple network from the host device. This may be accomplished in a number of ways. For example by joining the WiFi Management Access Point configured in initial setup, or by tethering from a Windows or Linux computer in an Internet Connection Sharing scenario as described in the previous chapter.

Once connected to the WiFi Pineapple network, browse to the *http://172.16.42.1:1471*

Note the *:1471* part of this URL. It's important to recognize that typically web servers operate on the default port 80 and do not require the port number to be specified in the browser with a colon after the IP address or hostname. The WiFi Pineapple web interface is hosted on the non-standard port 1471, and thus requires this addition to the URL.

It's important to also note that the WiFi Pineapple additionally runs a separate web server on port 80, for use in various attacks or as a landing page or captive portal to connected clients. For the most part outside of testing it's the *http://172.16.42.1:1471* address that you'll be interested in, so now is a good time to bookmark this page.

Lastly on browsers, it's a good idea to clear any cache associated with the 172.16.42.1 address, especially if you operate multiple WiFi Pineapples, update frequently or are upgrading from a previous model like the Mark V. The keyboard shortcut CTRL+SHIFT+DEL will bring up the clear browsing data menu in both Chrome and Firefox. Keep this in mind if you ever run into an instance where the web interface isn't behaving the way it should.

Elements of the Web Interface

The web interface is built on modern standards to be fast and responsive. While the majority of the page is dedicated to the specific module, some elements to note include the top bar, navigation bar and menu buttons.

The X icon from the top bar facilitates log-off, reboot and shutdown. If a notification is present, it will appear as a bell icon. Clicking the notification icon will show a list of notifications, which may be cleared. Notifications will also be listed from the dashboard.

The main navigation menu moderately follows the WiFi auditing workflow, listing system modules from Recon through Reporting. Of note, the Modules entry expands to list all installed user modules as well as the module manager.

Some tables, lists and sections are home to a menu button. Clicking this boxed down-arrow will expand options and additional functions. Some menus hook into the PineAP suite. For instance, clicking the menu button beside an SSID or MAC address listed in a Recon scan will provide SSID Pool and Filtering options. Other menus offer advanced functions such as downloading or clearing the SSID Pool.

Dashboard

The dashboard provides an at-a-glance view of the WiFi Pineapple status, landing page browser stats, notifications and bulletins.

Landing Page Browser Stats will display hits from popular web browsers when the Landing Page is enabled from Configuration. *Notifications* will display notifications from modules. The *Bulletins* feature fetches the latest project information from wifipineapple.com.

Clients

The WiFi Pineapple will allow clients to connect if Allow Associations is checked in PineAP. Connected clients will list in the Clients view along with their respective MAC Address, IP Address, the SSID to which they have connected (if Log Probes is enabled in PineAP) and Hostname. If the SSID or Hostname is unavailable it will display as such.

The Kick button allows the auditor to remove a client from the WiFi Pineapple network.

Clicking the menu button next to an MAC address shows a menu providing buttons to add or remove the MAC from the PineAP Filter or PineAP Tracking feature.

Clicking the menu button next to an SSID shows a menu providing buttons to add or remove the SSID from the PineAP Pool or PineAP Filter.

The Clients table can be updated by clicking the Refresh button.

Networking

From the Networking view, the auditor may make changes to the Routing, Access Point, MAC Addresses, Hostname and connect to an Access Point using WiFi Client Mode.

Route - The Kernel IP routing table is displayed and may be modified for the selected interface. The Route menu enables the auditor to Restart DNS. By default the expected Default Gateway is 172.16.42.42. When using the WiFi Pineapple Connector Android app, IP routing will automatically update to use `usb0` as the default gateway.

Access Point - The WiFi Pineapple primary open access point and management access point may be configured. Both the open and management access point share the same channel. The open access point may be hidden and the management access point may be disabled.

WiFi Client Mode - This feature enables the auditor to connect the WiFi Pineapple to another wireless access point for Internet or local network access. When using WiFi Client Mode, the IP routing will automatically update to use the selected interface. The WiFi Pineapple can be used with a number of supported USB WiFi adapters to add a third (wlan2) interface. wlan0 is reserved for use by the Access Point and wlan1 is required by PineAP and cannot be used if the PineAP Daemon and its subsequent features are being used.

To connect to a nearby Access Point, select the desired Interface and click Scan. From the Access Point list, choose the desired network, enter the Passphrase (if required) and click Connect. Once connected the WiFi Pineapple IP address will display and the Default Route will update to that of the newly connected network. Click Disconnect to end the connection.

MAC Address - The Current MAC address for the selected interface will display. A New MAC address may be specified manually, or set randomly using the New MAC text field and Set New MAC or Set Random MAC buttons. MAC Addresses may be reset to default from the MAC Address menu button. Changing MAC addresses may disconnect connected clients from the WiFi Pineapple.

Advanced - The Hostname may be updated using the hostname text field and Update Hostname button. Wireless configuration may be reset using the Reset WiFi Config to Defaults option from the Advanced menu button. The output of ifconfig is displayed.

Configuration

The Configuration view provides the auditor with means to set general settings and modify the landing page.

General - Timezone settings is displayed and may be manually selected. The system password may be set. The WiFi Pineapple may be rebooted or reset to factory defaults from the General menu button.

Landing Page - When enabled, this feature will act as a captive portal. New clients connecting to the WiFi Pineapple will be forwarded to this landing page. Some client devices will automatically launch a browser to this page upon connection. Landing page browser stats will display on the dashboard. PHP and HTML are accepted. The Landing Page may only display if the WiFi Pineapple has an Internet connection.

Advanced

The Advanced view provides the auditor with information on system resources, USB devices, file system table, CSS and the ability to upgrade the WiFi Pineapple firmware.

Resources - Displays file system disk usage and memory. From the Resources menu button Page Caches may be dropped.

USB - Displays connected USB peripherals and allows the auditor to set the file system table (fstab). SD cards may be formatted from the USB menu button (NANO Only).

CSS - The WiFi Pineapple Web Interface stylesheet may be modified.

10
WiFi Pineapple Modules

The WiFi Pineapple is designed to be as modular as possible. Most sections of the web interface are in fact modules, which may be updated from time to time. In addition to the system modules included with the WiFi Pineapple, such as Recon, Clients and PineAP, the WiFi Pineapple supports community developed modules.

These community developed modules extend functionality by using the WiFi Pineapple API. Anyone can develop for the WiFi Pineapple using this API (learn more at wifipineapple.com).

System and Community modules come in two varieties - GUI (web interface) and CLI (console). GUI modules will show in the web interface under the Modules menu. CLI modules may be managed using the module command from the console.

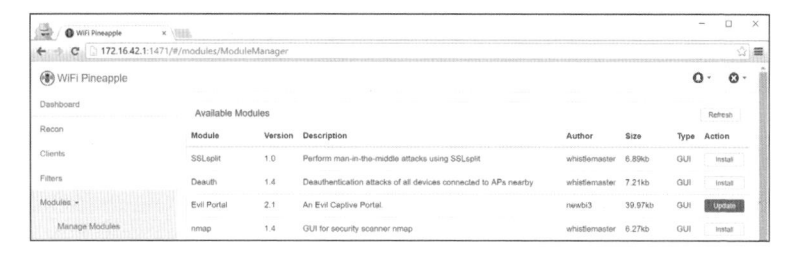

Modules may be managed (downloaded, updated, deleted) from the **Module Manager** section of the web interface.

Community developed modules are not required for successful operation of the WiFi Pineapple and come as-is with no warranty. Support is community driven and may be found from a modules section on the WiFi Pineapple forums. *https://www.wifipineapple.com/forum*

Module installation on the WiFi Pineapple NANO is recommended only to an external Micro SD card.

Modules are created with HTML, AngularJS and PHP, making requests and retrieving responses. Developers interested in creating these bootstrap-based modules may find in depth tutorials and API documentation from the WiFi Pineapple wiki at *wiki.wifipineapple.com*

Reconnaissance

The purpose of the Recon module is to see the big picture, gather intelligence, identify devices of interest and integrate with elements of the PineAP suite in order to conduct a targeted attack.

Unlike traditional War Driving, whereby the auditor passively listens for beacons being advertised by Access Points to paint a picture of the surrounding WiFi landscape, the WiFi Pineapple Recon goes one giant step further.

WiFi Pineapple Modules

By monitoring channels for both beacons and data activity, Recon paints a more complete picture by combining Access Points with their respective clients. With the WiFi landscape displayed in this

SSID	MAC	Security	Channel	Signal
GuestWiFi	00:C0:CA:8B:3B:26	Open	11	100%
	10:BF:48:BF:39:38			
	34:13:E8:25:FA:41			
	AC:CF:85:12:41:DE			
	C4:85:08:8F:72:E7			
The Network	10:BF:48:D8:60:67	WPA2	1	90%
acme-guest	00:1A:DD:C1:64:41	WPA2	1	60%
The Network Guest	10:BF:48:D8:60:67	WPA2	1	82%
ngHub_319445N90031A	E8:FC:AF:AE:9B:42	WPA2	11	48%
acme-n	00:1A:DD:C1:64:44	WPA2	1	58%
ATT568	B8:16:19:53:40:11	WPA2	1	28%
Sonic-391	60:FE:20:4D:AB:33	WPA2	2	24%

manner, a tester can quickly identify potential targets from Recon and immediately take action.

Recon allows the auditor to scan for nearby Access Points, or Access Points and their respective Clients. Clients are identified by sniffing for active traffic and are displayed underneath their parent Access Point. If a Client is associated to an Access Point but idle, it may not appear in the list. Increasing scan duration from the drop-down menu allows the sniffer to see more potential traffic on each channel.

The SSID, MAC, Security, Channel and Signal of Access Points are displayed in the table view. Clients are listed as MAC addresses only.

Clicking the menu button next to a MAC address shows a menu providing buttons to add or remove the MAC from the PineAP Filter or PineAP Tracking feature. Deauth uses the multiplier to send multiple deauthentication frames to the target Client. A multiplier of 2 is twice as many deauthentication frames as a multiplier of 1.

Clicking the menu button next to an SSID shows a menu providing buttons to add or remove the SSID from the PineAP Pool or PineAP Filter. Deauth Client will send deauthentication

WiFi Pineapple

frames to all associated clients currently recognized by Recon using the multiplier.

Unassociated Clients show in a unique table listed by MAC Address. These Clients have active radios, however are not associated to an Access Point.
Out Of Range Clients will display in a unique table along with their relationship to their parent Access Point by MAC address only.

Checking the Continuous box will enable an ongoing scan. The tables will update with the latest information from the scan duration interval until the scan is stopped.

Filtering

Filtering is essential to limiting the attack to the scope of engagement. Enabling the PineAP Allow Associations feature without a well crafted filter can result in unwanted casualties. Using intelligence gathered from the Recon view, as well as other open source techniques, the tester should build a robust filter specific to each audit.

Filtering may be performed by Client MAC Address or SSID. Both Deny and Allow modes are supported and this option may be toggled using the switch button.

Client Filtering

In Deny Mode, Clients with MAC Addresses listed in the Client Filter will not be able to connect to the WiFi Pineapple. In Allow Mode, only Clients with MAC Addresses listed in the Client Filter will be able to connect. When performing an audit, it is best to use Allow Mode to ensure that only clients within the scope of engagement are targeted.

Client MAC Addresses and SSIDs may be added from menu

buttons associated with their respective listings in Recon or Client views.

SSID Filtering

In Deny Mode, clients will not be able to associate with the WiFi Pineapple if they are attempting to connect to an SSID listed in the filter. In Allow Mode, clients will only be able to associate with the WiFi Pineapple if the SSID they are attempting to connect to is listed in the filter.

SSIDs may be added to the filter from the menu buttons associated with their respective listings in Recon.

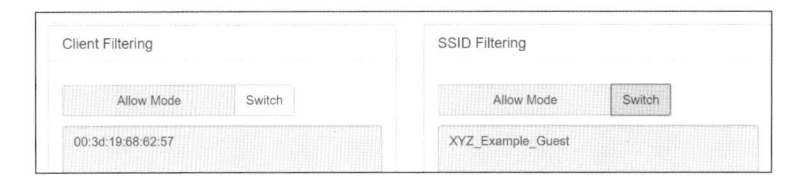

Client Filtering			SSID Filtering		
Allow Mode	Switch		Allow Mode	Switch	
00:3d:19:68:62:57			XYZ_Example_Guest		

Managing Filters

Filtered Clients and SSIDs will display in the lists. Client MAC addresses and SSIDs may be added to the list manually by using the text input field and Add button. Clicking a Client MAC or SSID will populate the text input field and clicking Remove will remove the entry from the Filter list.

Logs, Reporting & Analysis

Logs generate a plethora of valuable information. When analyzed, they can provide unique insights to the WiFi auditor such as device trends and preferred network lists. Logs compiled with reconnaissance augment reports, which may be generated continuously at set intervals for long term deployments.

Logging

In order to gather logs, they must first be enabled from the PineAP engine. Ensure that Log Probes and Log Associations are checked. When these passive sniffing features are enabled, SSIDs are captured from the probe requests of client devices. Associations to the WiFi Pineapple are logged along with their respective SSID.
The Logging view displays the PineAP Log, System Log, Dmesg and Reporting Log.

PineAP Log - Chronologically displays PineAP events if Log Probes and/or Log Associations are enabled. Each event contains a timestamp, event type (Probe Request or Association), the MAC address of the Client device, and the SSID for which the device is Probing or Associating.

Timestamp	Event	MAC	SSID
May 24 22:24:05	Probe Request	b8:44:d9:87:35:1b	xfinitywifi
May 24 22:24:17	Probe Request	e0:10:7f:15:d4:e8	Marriott
May 24 22:24:31	Probe Request	60:f1:89:20:92:2f	linksys
May 24 22:24:31	Probe Request	60:f1:89:20:92:2f	NETGEAR
May 24 22:24:31	Probe Request	60:f1:89:20:92:2f	default
May 24 22:24:31	Probe Request	50:7a:55:34:39:68	FreeWifi

PineAP Log Filtering - The Display Probes and Display Associations checkboxes enable the auditor to toggle the display of Probes or Associations. The Remove Duplicates checkbox will remove any duplicate entry, regardless of timestamp. For example, if a Client transmits a Probe Request for SSID "example" 10 times in 1 hour, checking the Remove Duplicates box will show only the first entry.

Filtering by MAC address and SSID is supported by completing the associated text fields. For example, if de:ad:be:ef:c0:fe is input in the MAC text field, only that Client device activity will show in the PineAP Log. Similarly the Log may be filtered by SSID.

WiFi Pineapple Modules

Filters do not apply until the Apply Filter button is pressed.
Clear Filter will reset to the default and display all captured data.
Refresh Log will obtain the latest log data from PineAP and Clear Log will empty the Log File.

Download Log - Logs may be downloaded from the web interface as a pineap.log file. This ascii text file contains a comma tab delimited list of all events including timestamp, MAC address and SSID. When used in conjunction with the log analysis script, trends may be determined.

Log Location - by default the PineAP log is saved in the volatile /tmp/ directory. Upon reboot, all data will be lost. Changing this value will enable the WiFi auditor to maintain log files even after reboots.

Reporting

This feature enables the auditor to generate reports at a specified interval. The report may be sent via email and/or saved locally on a suitable SD card (NANO only). See the Format SD Card option from the USB menu on the Advanced view to setup a new card. Email Configuration must be complete in order for the Send Report via email function to operate successfully.
The Report Contents may contain: the PineAP Log with an option to clear after generating the report, a PineAP Site Survey similar to the Recon View with option to specify AP & Client scan duration, and PineAP Probing and Tracked Clients.

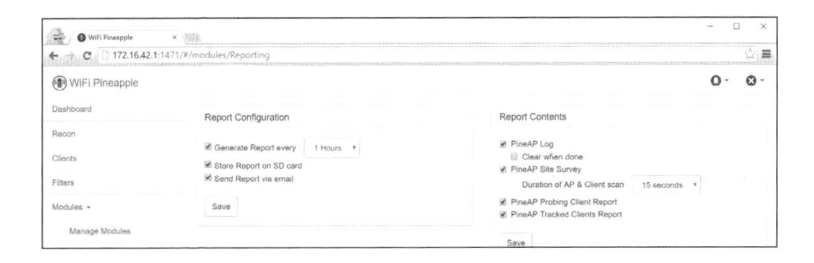

71

Analysis

One simple way to analyze the PineAP log is to use the built-in filtering options. By entering the MAC address of an interesting client device, all probed for SSIDs may be revealed. Similarly, by filtering for SSID, all interested client devices may be revealed by MAC address. This is immensely valuable when developing filters for a specific engagement.

For a more general analysis of trends from a log, an analysis script is provided. Downloadable from *https://www.wifipineapple.com/analyze.sh*, this script will accept a PineAP log as its input. When run, the script will check download the latest OUI database from IEEE and check it against the provided PineAP log. Unique probe requests, devices and OUIs will list along with the top device manufacturers found in the log.

Tracking Clients

The tracking feature will continuously scan for specified Clients by MAC address and execute a customizable Tracking Script. This feature requires the Log Probes and/or Log Associations features of PineAP to be enabled.
Clients may be specified manually using the text field and add button. Clients may also be added to the Client Tracking List by using the PineAP Tracking Add MAC button from an associated MAC address within the Clients view or Recon view. Selecting a MAC address from the Client Tracking List will populate the text field for removal using the Remove button.

When a client is identified by a logged Probe or Association, the customizable Tracking Script will execute. The Tracking Script defines variables for the Client MAC address, the identification type (Probe or Association) and the SSID with which the Client is Probing or Associating.

11
Shell Access and Upgrades

The WiFi Pineapple platform is built on the OpenWRT distribution of the popular GNU/Linux ("Linux") operating system. Accessing the Linux console may provide the penetration tester with a familiar environment as both busybox (`/bin/sh`) and bash (`/bin/bash`) are included. Furthermore, packages may be installed from the opkg package management system.

> **NANO Note:** after running `opkg update`, install packages to the MicroSD card using the `--dest parameter`. Example: `opkg --dest sd install nmap`

Two WiFi Pineapple specific commands are provided to interface with PineAP and installed modules which support CLI functions: `pineapple` and `module`.

Secure Shell

The most common way to access the WiFi Pineapple console is via Secure Shell (SSH). SSH clients are preinstalled on most Linux and Mac systems. Windows users are advised to download a SSH utility such as the popular PuTTY client. Android users may also find compatible SSH clients from Google Play.

To connect to the WiFi Pineapple console over SSH, first connect to the WiFi Pineapple network from your host device. Once connected, ssh to the WiFi Pineapple IP address (default: 172.16.42.1) with the username root and password configured on setup. This is the same password as used to access the web interface. The SSH service on the WiFi Pineapple operates at the default port 22.

```
ssh root@172.16.42.1
```

Serial

Convenient access to the WiFi Pineapple TETRA serial console is provided by its USB UART port. From this console you can access the WiFi Pineapple command line, which is useful for operation from the CLI commands pineapple and module.

Linux Hosts

When connected to a Linux host PC via USB cable, the device will enumerate as a usbserial device. After connecting the USB cable, check the output of `dmesg | grep tty` to determine the device name. It will typically enumerate as `ttyUSB0`.

From your preferred console, access the serial device using the following settings:

```
flowcontrol: none
baudrate: 115200
parity: none
databits: 8
stopbit: 1
```

Shell Access and Upgrades

For example, with picocom execute `picocom -b 115200 /dev/ttyUSB0` or screen execute `screen /dev/ttyUSB0 115200`.

Once connected you must press ENTER to activate the console. Login as root with the password configured at setup.

Windows Hosts

When connecting to a Windows host, open Device Manager and check for the new USB Serial Port (COM#) device under Ports (COM & LPT). Then using PuTTY, select Serial under Connection Type, enter the COM# under Serial Line and 115200 under Speed and click Open. *http://www.putty.org/*

Once connected you must press ENTER to activate the console. Login as root with the password configured at setup.

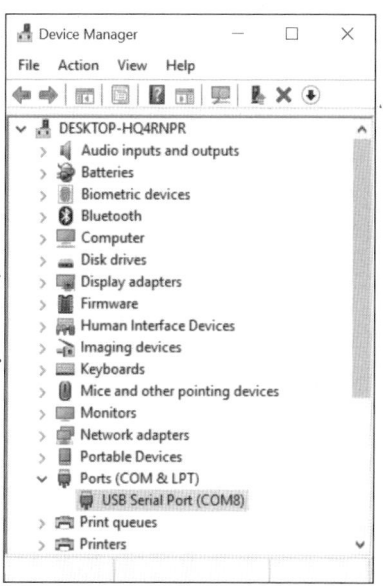

Note: If Windows does not automatically install the Microsoft WHQL serial driver from Windows Update, you may download it from FTDI at *http://www.ftdichip.com/Drivers/D2XX.htm*

Upgrading the Firmware

Many feature upgrades come in the form of Modules to be installed and updated over the air. Other, typically lower level features, require firmware upgrades. As the WiFi Pineapple platform continues to develop, firmware updates will become available.

75

Firmware updates may be checked from the Advanced menu.

Firmware Upgrade - Displays current firmware version and allows the auditor to check for updates. This requires an Internet connection and will initiate a connection to *WiFiPineapple.com*. If an update is available, the changelog will display and the option to Perform Upgrade will be available. Users are advised to carefully read the warnings related to the firmware upgrade feature.

Warning

Firmware upgrades replace all data (excluding external storage such as SD card or USB). Please ensure any important non-system data has been backed up.

Please stop any unnecessary services and modules before upgrading. Restarting the WiFi Pineapple without starting additional services and modules is recommended to ensure extra processes have been halted properly.

Upgrading firmware should only be done while using a stable power source. An Ethernet connection to the WiFi Pineapple is recommended for this process.

Once the firmware upgrade has completed the WiFi Pineapple will reboot into an initial setup state. This process will take several minutes. Do not interrupt the upgrade process by unplugging power or closing the web interface as this may result in a soft-brick state.

```
 /)___(\
 (=' . '=)
 (")_(")
```
EOF